Collins

easy learning

Fractions

Ages 5–7

$\dfrac{3}{4}$

$\dfrac{1}{4}$

Adam Blackwood
Melissa Blackwood

How to use this book

- Find a quiet, comfortable place to work, away from other distractions.

- Tackle one topic at a time.

- Help with reading the instructions where necessary, and ensure that your child understands what to do.

- Help and encourage your child to check their own answers as they complete each activity.

- Discuss with your child what they have learnt.

- Let your child return to their favourite pages once they have been completed, to talk about the activities.

- Reward your child with plenty of praise and encouragement.

Special features

- Yellow boxes: Introduce and outline the key ideas in each section.

- Orange shaded boxes: Offer advice to parents on how to consolidate your child's understanding.

Published by Collins
An imprint of HarperCollins*Publishers*
1 London Bridge Street
London SE1 9GF

Browse the complete Collins catalogue at
www.collins.co.uk

© HarperCollins*Publishers* 2011
This edition © HarperCollins*Publishers* 2015

11

ISBN 978-0-00-813444-0

The author and publisher are grateful to the copyright holders for permission to use the quoted materials and images.

p9 and 32 © vector_ann/ shutterstock.com
p29 © Coprid/ shutterstock.com

Printed in Great Britain by Bell and Bain Ltd, Glasgow

The authors assert their moral right to be identified as the authors of this work.

British Library Cataloguing in Publication Data

A Catalogue record for this publication is available from the British Library

Written by Adam Blackwood and Melissa Blackwood
Page design by QBS Learning
Cover illustration © Zygotehaasnobrain/shutterstock.com
Cover design by Sarah Duxbury and Paul Oates
Project managed by Andy Slater

MIX
Paper from
responsible sources
FSC
www.fsc.org
FSC™ C007454

Contents

What is a fraction?

If you have the **whole** of something, you have all of it, for example, a **whole** apple.

A fraction is when the whole is **split** into **equal parts**.

1 Draw a line between each label and the correct picture.

A whole bunch of bananas

A whole purse of coins

A whole football

A whole lollipop

The whole world

A whole glass of juice

4

2 Look at the following. Add a tick (✓) if it is a fraction, a cross (✗) if it is not.

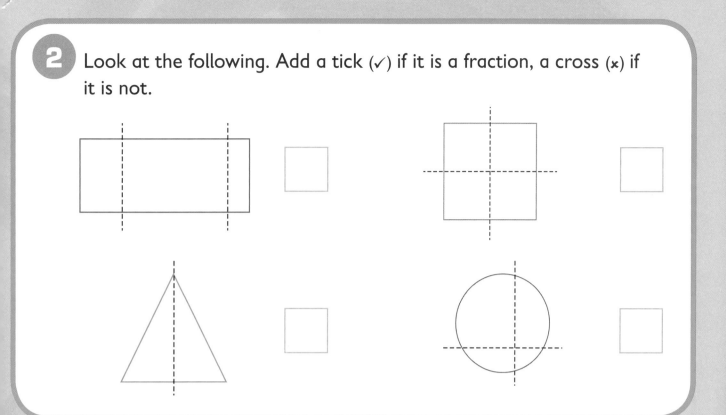

3

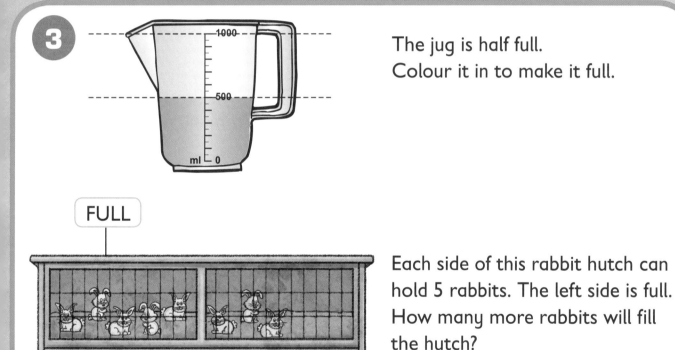

The jug is half full.
Colour it in to make it full.

FULL

Each side of this rabbit hutch can hold 5 rabbits. The left side is full. How many more rabbits will fill the hutch?

◻ rabbits

Writing fractions

A fraction is written as two numbers, one above the other, with a line between them, for example $\frac{1}{2}$, $\frac{1}{3}$, $\frac{1}{4}$

A pizza is cut into **4** equal pieces. Each piece is a quarter, $\frac{1}{4}$

$\frac{1}{4}$

The top number shows how many pieces of pizza each person has.

The bottom number shows how many pieces the pizza was cut into altogether.

---

1 For each picture, write how many pieces of pizza one child would get.

2 Write these fractions in numbers.

one-half ☐

one-quarter ☐

one-third ☐

two-quarters ☐

3 In each picture, one whole fruit has been shared fairly between these children. Look at how many pieces of fruit each child has. Complete the fraction in each sentence.

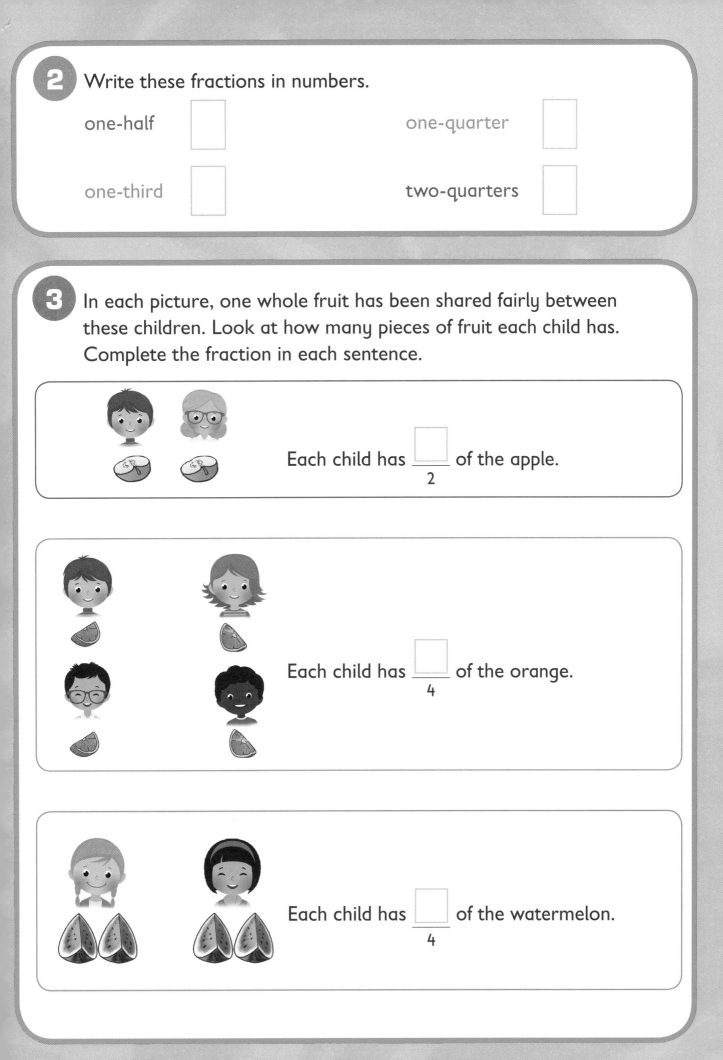

Each child has ☐/2 of the apple.

Each child has ☐/4 of the orange.

Each child has ☐/4 of the watermelon.

Halves

One-half is written like this, $\frac{1}{2}$

This means **one whole** shared into **two equal parts**, and **one-half** is one of those parts.

When objects are shared in half, two people get exactly the same number.

For example, if a block of **8** squares of chocolate is shared equally between **2** children, both children get **4** squares.

1 Colour half of each object or shape. Write one-half in numbers next to each one.

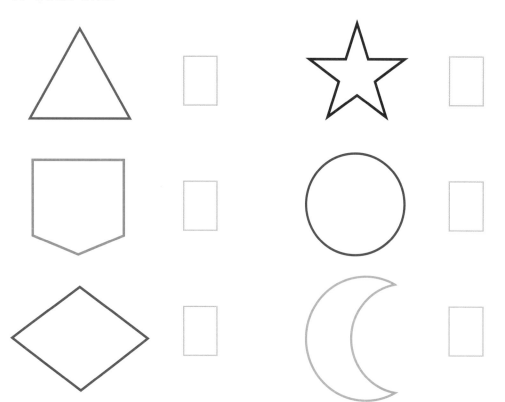

Talk to your child about objects you notice around you in real life that can be exactly shared in half. It is important to make sure they understand one-half is an exact amount.

2 Draw a line through each bar of chocolate to cut into halves.

3 Share each of these in half. Write the correct number in each answer box.

How many oranges for each basket? ☐ oranges

How many cherries for each bowl of ice cream? ☐ cherries

How many children for each roundabout? ☐ children

Quarters

One-quarter is written like this, $\frac{1}{4}$

This means **one whole** shared into **four equal parts**, and **one-quarter** is one of those parts.

For example, if **8** balloons were shared fairly between **4** children, each child would get **2** balloons.

$\frac{1}{4}$ $\frac{1}{4}$ $\frac{1}{4}$ $\frac{1}{4}$

There are **4** children, each getting an equal share.
$\frac{1}{4}$ of **8** balloons is **2** balloons.

---

1 Colour one-quarter of each shape. Write one-quarter in numbers next to each one.

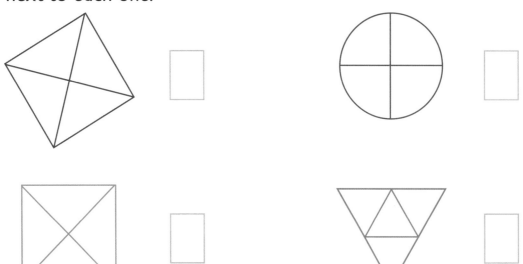

2 Divide the flag into four quarters. Draw a different coloured circle in each quarter.

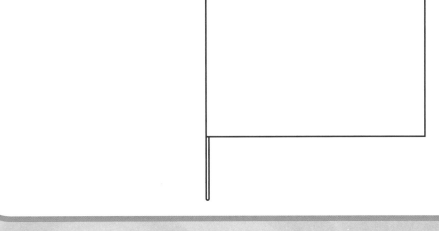

3 Share these 12 balloons fairly between 4 children.
Draw the number of balloons each child receives.
Then, write the fraction that each child has.

4 Share the 8 ice cream scoops so each bowl has the same number.
Draw the correct number of scoops in each bowl.

Thirds

One-third is written like this, $\frac{1}{3}$

This means **one whole** shared into **three equal parts**, and **one-third** is one of those parts.

For example, **6** sweets shared fairly between **3** children would give them **2** each.

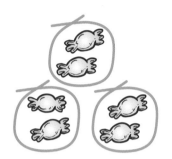

---

1 Colour one-third of each shape. Write one-third in numbers next to each one.

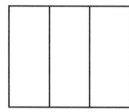

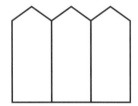

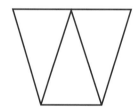

---

2 Draw a path across the maze by going through all of the pictures, symbols or words that show one-third. You can move in any direction, including diagonally.

Start →

$\frac{1}{3}$			$\frac{1}{4}$			one quarter
one half		one third		one half		$\frac{1}{3}$
	$\frac{1}{2}$				one third	

3 In a vase, one-third of flowers are pink, one-third are yellow and one-third are red. Finish colouring the flowers.

A lady picks one-third of the flowers from the vase.
How many flowers does she pick?

 flowers

4 Each nest has the same number of eggs in it. How many eggs are in each nest?

 eggs

Make sure your child understands that the use of 'third' in 'one-third' is different to its use in 'third place' in a race.

Counting halves

We know that halves are **one whole** shared into **two equal parts**. One of these equal parts is one-half.

If you start with more than one whole, you can have more than two-halves.

For example, **3** apples cut into halves give **6** halves.

1 How many halves are there in each row?

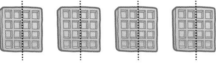

_____ halves

_____ halves

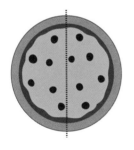 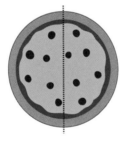

_____ halves

_____ halves

A great way of practising counting using the word 'half' in real life is when you take your child shopping for shoes. Count along the sizes together, until you find their correct size.

2 These items will be cut into halves. How many halves will there be in each row?

_____ halves

_____ halves

_____ halves

3 We can use a number sequence to count in halves. We add or take away a half to get the next number in the sequence.
Like this:

$+\dfrac{1}{2}$ $+\dfrac{1}{2}$ $+\dfrac{1}{2}$ $+\dfrac{1}{2}$ $+\dfrac{1}{2}$ $+\dfrac{1}{2}$ $+\dfrac{1}{2}$

1 $1\dfrac{1}{2}$ 2 $2\dfrac{1}{2}$ 3 $3\dfrac{1}{2}$ 4 $4\dfrac{1}{2}$

Complete these number sequences.

$+\dfrac{1}{2}$ $+\dfrac{1}{2}$ $+\dfrac{1}{2}$

$6\dfrac{1}{2}$ 7 $7\dfrac{1}{2}$ ☐   ☐   ☐   ☐   ☐

$-\dfrac{1}{2}$ $-\dfrac{1}{2}$ $-\dfrac{1}{2}$

8 $7\dfrac{1}{2}$ 7 ☐   ☐   ☐   ☐   ☐

When preparing a snack or meal for a group of people, include your child in the preparations, asking questions like those in question 2.

Counting quarters

We know that quarters are **one whole** shared into **four equal parts**. One of these equal parts is one-quarter.

If you start with more than one whole, you can have more than four-quarters. For example, **2** pizzas cut into quarters give **8** quarters.

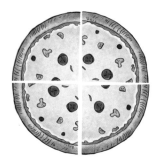 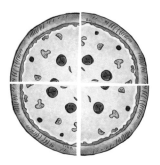

1 Write how many quarters of sandwich there are in each picture.

 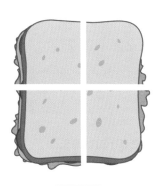 

2 These glasses of orange juice are marked in quarters. Write as a fraction how much juice is in each glass.

3 These jellies will be cut into quarters. Each quarter of a jelly needs one bowl to go in. How many bowls are needed?

      bowls

4 We can use a number sequence to count in quarters. We add or take away a quarter to get the next number in the sequence.
Like this:

$+\frac{1}{4}$ $+\frac{1}{4}$ $+\frac{1}{4}$ $+\frac{1}{4}$ $+\frac{1}{4}$

1 $1\frac{1}{4}$ $1\frac{2}{4}$ $1\frac{3}{4}$ 2 $2\frac{1}{4}$

Complete these number sequences.

$+\frac{1}{4}$ $+\frac{1}{4}$ $+\frac{1}{4}$

3 $3\frac{1}{4}$ $3\frac{2}{4}$ ☐ ☐ ☐ ☐ ☐

$+\frac{1}{4}$ $+\frac{1}{4}$ $+\frac{1}{4}$

$8\frac{1}{4}$ $8\frac{2}{4}$ $8\frac{3}{4}$ ☐ ☐ ☐ ☐ ☐

$-\frac{1}{4}$ $-\frac{1}{4}$ $-\frac{1}{4}$

6 $5\frac{3}{4}$ $5\frac{2}{4}$ ☐ ☐ ☐ ☐ ☐

To see how your child understands fractions, you can draw a line, with 0 at one end and 1 at the other. Ask them to mark on where $\frac{1}{4}$, $\frac{2}{4}$ and $\frac{3}{4}$ would be. They should be the same distance apart.

Counting thirds

We know that thirds are **one whole** shared into **three equal parts**. One of these equal parts is one-third.

If you start with more than one whole, you can have more than three-thirds. For example, **2** pancakes cut into thirds give **6** thirds.

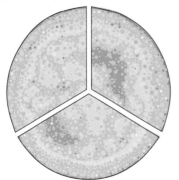 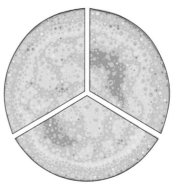

1 Write in thirds how much ice cream is in each tub.

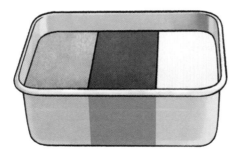

_____ thirds or I whole

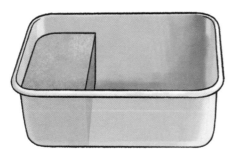

_____ third

_____ thirds

2 These items will be cut into thirds. How many thirds will there be in each row?

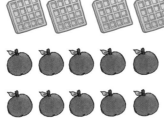

_____ thirds

_____ thirds

_____ thirds

3 We can use a number sequence to count in thirds. We add or take away a third to get the next number in the sequence.
Like this:

$$+\frac{1}{3} \quad +\frac{1}{3} \quad +\frac{1}{3} \quad +\frac{1}{3}$$

$$1 \qquad 1\frac{1}{3} \qquad 1\frac{2}{3} \qquad 2 \qquad 2\frac{1}{3}$$

Complete these number sequences.

$$+\frac{1}{3} \qquad +\frac{1}{3} \qquad +\frac{1}{3}$$

$$2 \qquad 2\frac{1}{3} \qquad 2\frac{2}{3} \quad \square \quad \square \quad \square \quad \square \quad \square$$

$$+\frac{1}{3} \qquad +\frac{1}{3} \qquad +\frac{1}{3}$$

$$7\frac{2}{3} \qquad 8 \qquad 8\frac{1}{3} \quad \square \quad \square \quad \square \quad \square$$

$$-\frac{1}{3} \qquad -\frac{1}{3} \qquad -\frac{1}{3}$$

$$5\frac{2}{3} \qquad 5\frac{1}{3} \qquad 5 \quad \square \quad \square \quad \square \quad \square \quad \square$$

Help your child link thirds to the three times table by counting objects in threes. Share objects into three groups and show how each group is one-third of the total number of objects.

Fractions around the clock

We use fractions when we tell the time.

There are 15 minutes in a
quarter of an hour.

There are 30 minutes in a
half an hour.

There are 60 minutes in a
whole hour.

o'clock

quarter
to

quarter
past

half past

1 These clocks only show the minute hand. Draw the new
position of the minute hand after **half** an hour has passed.
The first one has been done for you.

20

2 Read the sentence and write **true** or **false** in the answer box.

A half of the clock face has been coloured yellow.

A quarter of the clock face has been coloured yellow.

A half of the clock face has been coloured yellow.

A quarter of the clock face has been coloured yellow.

3 The hands on these clocks split the clock faces into halves.
Draw another line to split each clock face into quarters.
The first one has been done for you.

Divide this clock into quarters in another way.

When talking about the time with your child, point out that the clock face is divided into four quarters. Starting from 'o'clock', 'quarter past' is one-quarter of the way round the clock face, 'half past' is half the way round and 'quarter to' is three-quarters of the way round.

Turning around

On this page you will learn about turning **quarter** or **half** of a circle.

Look at this big wheel.

You can get on, go all the way round once, then get off – one full turn.

If you go to the top, you are halfway round.

You may only go a quarter of the way round before the ride stops.

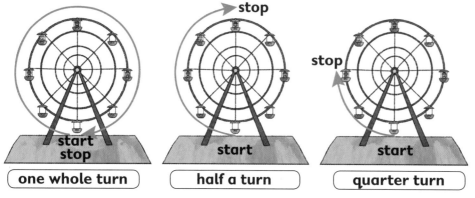

| one whole turn | half a turn | quarter turn |

Turns can be **clockwise** or **anticlockwise**.

anticlockwise   clockwise

---

1 Colour in the windmill to show it has turned half a turn.

Colour in the windmill to show it has turned a quarter turn clockwise.

Colour in the windmill to show it has turned a whole turn.

2 Face a wall. Follow these instructions in order. Write down which direction you are facing when you have finished.

> 1. Turn halfway round → 2. Turn a quarter clockwise

> 4. Turn halfway round ← 3. Turn a quarter anticlockwise

I am facing _____

---

3 Write instructions for Anna to find her way home.
The first one has been done for you.

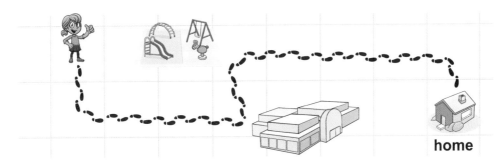

home

1 Forward 1 square. Quarter turn anticlockwise.

2 _____

3 _____

4 _____

5 _____

Equivalent fractions

Look at these two flags. Two of the quarters have been coloured on one flag and half has been coloured on the other. These are the same amounts. We call them **equivalent**.

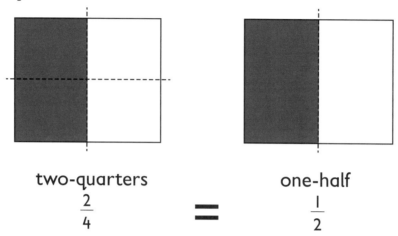

two-quarters

$\frac{2}{4}$

=

one-half

$\frac{1}{2}$

1 Colour the second flag so that the two flags are equivalent. Write the fractions next to each flag.

2 Write the fraction of the coloured part of each shape.
Circle any fractions that are equivalent.

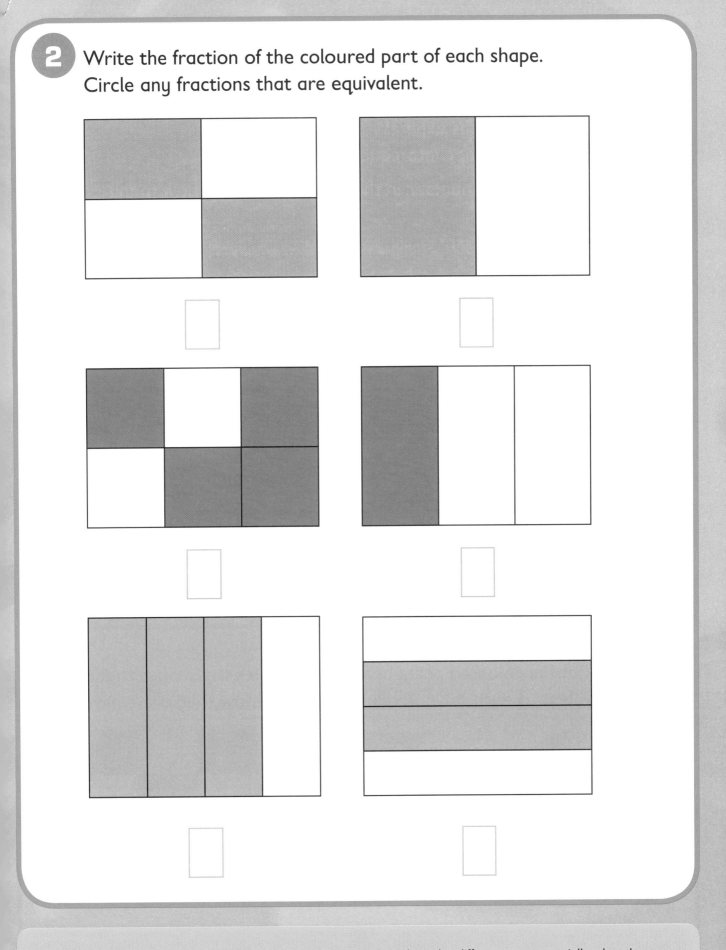

Some children can struggle with the idea that half a shape can be coloured in different ways, especially when the coloured parts are not neatly next to each other. Questions like this are common in tests to see if children understand that fractions are equal parts.

Fractions of shapes

You are almost a fractions expert!
You can now share a shape into equal parts.

Remember that the top number in the fraction tells you how many of these equal parts you have.

1 Circle the bigger fraction. Explain how you know which is bigger.

$\frac{3}{4}$ 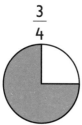 $\frac{1}{2}$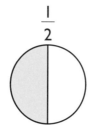

I know this fraction is bigger because

_____

_____

1 whole $\frac{3}{4}$

I know this fraction is bigger because

_____

_____

2 Look at the coloured parts of the shapes. Tick the shapes that are equivalent to each other. Explain how you know they are equivalent.

I know these fractions are the equivalent because _____

_____

3 Colour half of the squares in each of these shapes.
Use a different pattern of squares for each one.

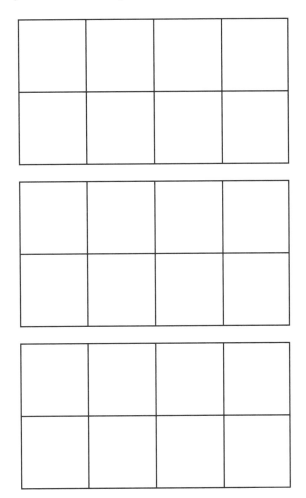

4 Colour half of each shape. Do not colour in two parts that are next to each other.

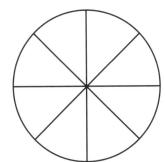 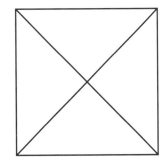 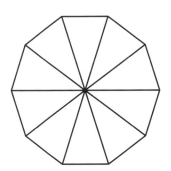

'Reasoning' or being able to explain your thinking is an important skill. If a child is able to explain how they arrived at an answer, they will have a deeper understanding than a child that says they 'just know'.

Putting it into practice

Use your knowledge of fractions to solve these real-life problems.

1 Half of these coins belong to your friend. How many are left over?

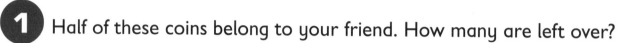

_____ coins

2 One-third of your button collection is shown below. Draw the rest of your buttons in the box.

There are _____ buttons altogether.

Can you colour one-third of your buttons green?

3 Slices of pineapple, watermelon, lime and orange have been cut into quarters. How many whole slices of each fruit did I start with?

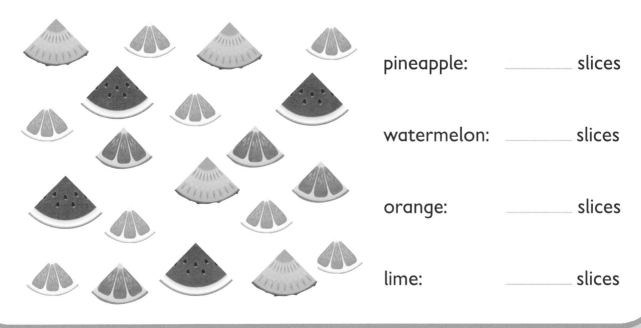

pineapple: _____ slices

watermelon: _____ slices

orange: _____ slices

lime: _____ slices

4 Join each fraction to the correct picture.

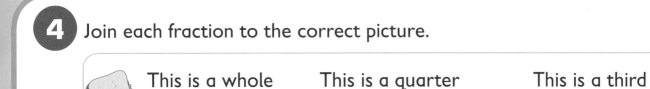

This is a whole sandwich   This is a quarter of a sandwich   This is a third of a sandwich

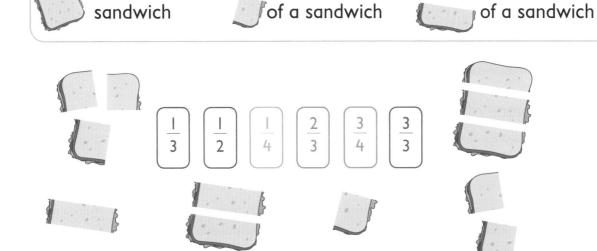

$\frac{1}{3}$ $\frac{1}{2}$ $\frac{1}{4}$ $\frac{2}{3}$ $\frac{3}{4}$ $\frac{3}{3}$

5 What is half of 20 centimetres (cm)?

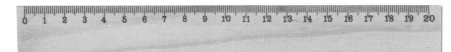

Putting it into practice

6 A ladybird has 14 spots. Draw the spots on the ladybird so that half are on each wing.

7 What is one-third of 30 millilitres (ml)?

_____

8 This piece of string measures 40 cm. How long is one-quarter of it?

0   10   20   30   40 cm

_____

9 I need six eggs for a recipe. Is three-quarters of this box of eggs enough? Circle yes or no.

| yes | no |

10 A full box of bananas has 12 bananas in it.

A monkey eats $\frac{1}{3}$ of a box of bananas every day.
How many bananas does he eat in a day? _____

The box has $\frac{2}{3}$ of the bananas left in it.
How many bananas are left? _____

11 Birdwatchers watched a bird feeding table for a day.
They saw 12 birds. They were all sparrows or blackbirds.
Complete the table.

Bird	Fraction	Number seen
Sparrow	$\frac{3}{4}$	
Blackbird	$\frac{1}{4}$	

12 There are 16 teams in a football tournament.
Half the teams are wearing **red** shirts, one-quarter are wearing
green shirts and one-quarter are wearing **blue** shirts.
Colour the shirts to show how many teams wear each colour.

A great way of practising fractions is through cooking or baking. Ask your child for a 'third of a box of eggs' or 'half of the amount of flour in the recipe', depending on the level of understanding they have.

Answers

Page 4

What is a fraction?

1

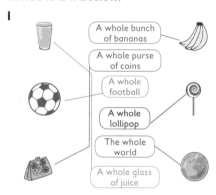

A whole bunch of bananas
A whole purse of coins
A whole football
A whole lollipop
The whole world
A whole glass of juice

Page 5

2 Rectangle – (✗)   Square – (✓)
  Triangle – (✓)   Circle – (✗)
3 Full jug shaded
  2 more rabbits

Page 6

Writing fractions

1 For each question, each child would get 1 piece.

Page 7

2 one-half = $\frac{1}{2}$ one-quarter = $\frac{1}{4}$

  one-third = $\frac{1}{3}$ two-quarters = $\frac{2}{4}$

3 $\frac{1}{2}$ of apple $\frac{1}{4}$ of orange

  $\frac{2}{4}$ of watermelon

Page 8

Halves

1 Answers will vary. Half of each shape should be coloured.

  $\frac{1}{2}$ for all shapes.

Page 9

2 Just one line is required. The square bar could also be split from corner to corner.

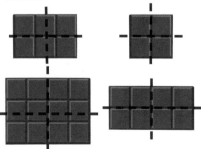

3 5 oranges, 6 cherries, 3 children

Page 10

Quarters

1 Answers will vary. One part of each shape should be coloured.

  $\frac{1}{4}$ for all shapes.

Page 11

2 Answers will vary.

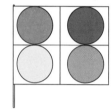

3 3 balloons each;

  $\frac{1}{4}$ of the total each

4 Each bowl to have 2 scoops of ice cream drawn.

Page 12

Thirds

1 Answers will vary. One part of each shape should be coloured.

  $\frac{1}{3}$ for all shapes.

2

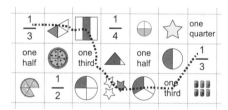

Page 13

3

  Answers will vary. There should be 3 of each colour.
  3 flowers
4 2 eggs

Page 14

Counting halves

1 8 halves, 14 halves, 4 halves, 12 halves

Page 15

2 10 halves   6 halves   20 halves

(top right)

3 $6\frac{1}{2}$, 7, $7\frac{1}{2}$, 8, $8\frac{1}{2}$, 9, $9\frac{1}{2}$, 10

  8, $7\frac{1}{2}$, 7, $6\frac{1}{2}$, 6, $5\frac{1}{2}$, 5, $4\frac{1}{2}$

Page 16

Counting quarters

1 3, 4, 1

2 $\frac{1}{4}$, $\frac{2}{4}$ or $\frac{1}{2}$, $\frac{3}{4}$

Page 17

3 20 bowls

4 3, $3\frac{1}{4}$, $3\frac{2}{4}$, $3\frac{3}{4}$, 4, $4\frac{1}{4}$, $4\frac{2}{4}$, $4\frac{3}{4}$

  $8\frac{1}{4}$, $8\frac{2}{4}$, $8\frac{3}{4}$, 9, $9\frac{1}{4}$, $9\frac{2}{4}$, $9\frac{3}{4}$, 10

  6, $5\frac{3}{4}$, $5\frac{2}{4}$, $5\frac{1}{4}$, 5, $4\frac{3}{4}$, $4\frac{2}{4}$, $4\frac{1}{4}$

Page 18

Counting thirds

1 3 thirds; 1 third; 2 thirds

Page 19

2 12 thirds, 30 thirds, 9 thirds

3 2, $2\frac{1}{3}$, $2\frac{2}{3}$, 3, $3\frac{1}{3}$, $3\frac{2}{3}$, 4, $4\frac{1}{3}$

  $7\frac{2}{3}$, 8, $8\frac{1}{3}$, $8\frac{2}{3}$, 9, $9\frac{1}{3}$, $9\frac{2}{3}$, 10

  $5\frac{2}{3}$, $5\frac{1}{3}$, 5, $4\frac{2}{3}$, $4\frac{1}{3}$, 4, $3\frac{2}{3}$, $3\frac{1}{3}$

Page 20

Fractions around the clock

1

Page 21

2 True   False   False   True

3